WHERE'S MY **TEEN ??**

BRINGING OUR TEENAGERS CLOSER, ONE STEP AT A TIME

Dr. B B AGRAWAL, MD

BlueRose ONE.com
Stories Matter
NewDelhi • London

BLUEROSE PUBLISHERS
India | U.K.

BlueRose ONE.com
Stories Matter
NewDelhi • London

For permission requests or inquiries regarding this publication,
please contact:

BLUEROSE PUBLISHERS
www.BlueRoseONE.com
info@bluerosepublishers.com
+91 8882 898 898
+4407342408967

ISBN: 978-93-6783-788-7

Cover Design: AdPrayas, Chhattisgarh, India
Typesetting: Sagar

First Edition: January 2025

Appreciation for the book

As a tree is known by the fruit it bears, so it is the case with parents. As a tree helps its flowers to turn into ripe fruits, so it is the duty of parents tohelp, the children evolve into wonderful, responsible and sincere citizens. This book is a great savior for many parents,including me. Dr Agrawal has offered practical tips from his own rich experience of counseling numerous parents.

As an academician, I wouldalso recommend this book to all the parents whose children are studying in our schools.

Dr Kiranpal Singh Chawla

Chairperson

Arpa River Valley International School, Bilaspur

HSM Global Public School, Bilaspur

My Gratitude to

My respected parents
(for bringing me up as you have)

Shweta – my wife
(my best friend & companion)

Ayam - our son
(my second-best friend & companion)

My revered teachers
My dear friends & classmates
(School, MBBS, MD)

My dear co-teachers & volunteers
(Shiv Shakti Centre)

My patients & workshop participants
(the learning has been mutual)

&

Param Poojya Gurudev Sri Sri Ravishankar Ji

(For taking us into your fold)

(Showering with your unconditional love)

(Guiding into the path of wisdom)

(Taking care of what has been, is & will be)

❶

For **parents,**

Teenage is when **teenagers** become difficult

&

For **teenagers,**

Teenage is when **parents** become difficult

****

❷

"It is not the mountains we conquer, but ourselves."

- Sir Edmund Hillary

****

Table of Contents

Before we begin

Hello dear friend,

- Are you a parent to a teenage son or daughter
- And are you facing issues with them?
- Looking for genuine solutions?
- Do you feel your teenager needs guidance?
- And you need help for that!!

Then this book is for you.

And I feel happy to welcome you on this journey with me, the journey of nurturing teens in today's tough world.

The book is written for parents with an aim of bringing about a welcome change in your & your teen's lives & perspective.

As parents & caregivers, our aim is to nurture our young ones into strong, self-sufficient grownups, capable not only of taking their own responsibility, but also supporting us when the time comes.

When they can manage life without our help, confidently make their own decisions, and overcome challenges with courage, we know we've done a great job as parents.

And the chapters in this book are structured with this very aim in mind, to take you on a step-by-step journey through your teenage son & daughter's life & struggles & improve your understanding & bonding.

And therefore, it's best to go through the chapters in their sequence. Yet, if you feel tempted to jump directly to a chapter which has caught your attention, that's fine, but thereafter, also go through the chapters in sequence, to get a complete experience & optimum benefit. Because this book is more than just a book, it's a carefully designed journey. And please don't rush to read all the chapters at one go. Go slow. Read one chapter at a time, introspect, discuss with your spouse, apply the lessons. And then proceed for the next one.

As you progress through this journey, you'll uncover profound insights, for you and your teenager, to win over the hurdles you would be facing. And, to make the process even more effective:

- there are activities & assignments for you
- you will be asked to introspect & note down what comes up
- there will be blank pages for putting your thoughts & observations (or you may use a diary or notebook for these)

Because, you see:

- Just reading & appreciating doesn't change much, but
- taking action does, &
- That's the aim of this book - a quick, long-lasting, positive change in your & your teens' life.

So, let's:

- treasure the present moments while they're still young,
- accept their shortcomings,
- celebrate their strengths,
- understand their struggles,
- & help them in the best way we can.

Together, we can guide them on this beautiful journey of life to become strong, capable, loving adults. And we should.

I share what I have learned from life - my own / my patients / my workshop participants.

My best wishes for your life journey & welcome again.

In the first chapter itself, we will begin with a powerful concept for conflict resolution & nurturing great relationships with our teenagers that I have successfully applied in my life. I am confident you too will find it very useful. Best wishes.

Dr Banke Bihari Agrawal

MD (Pediatrics)

24 Sept 2024

Chapter 1

Let's begin with an intense idea!!

The teenage years can be fun and exciting for your teenage son and daughter, but they can also be frustrating and stressful for you as a parent.

Almost every parent (of a teenager) goes through a roller coaster of emotions - from feeling love and pride for their teen to feeling puzzled and annoyed to feeling outright frustrated & helpless. You need unlimited patience when dealing with your teens.

Here, I share with you a profound idea for building strong relationships, which I have applied in my life. This concept works for all relationships, including those between you and your teens. The concept is:

YOU & YOUR CHILDREN ARE ONE TEAM

Sounds simple! Let's see.

I believe that a parent's victory doesn't lie in dominating over their children, but in bridging your differences with them and fostering an honest, intense relationship based on trust, respect and open communication.

What do you say?

My journey (personal as well as professional) has taught me that we and our children are not opponents, but rather, we're one team.

It's not about one of you winning & the other conceding defeat, & not even about settling for a draw as far as possible (Draw means a compromise; & it is needed at times).

It's about both sides winning & winning together, as far as possible, & creating a loving and lasting bond. You don't always have to fight against each other; rather, together, as a team, you have to fight against your differences, for a WIN-WIN.

Like everyone, I too have had my fair share of conflicts with my son, spouse, and friends. And as happens to everyone, ego, anger, and frustration often took over me during those times. But no matter how much I fretted, in the end, I had to fall back on the **"ONE TEAM"** mantra, had to remind myself that we are one team and only then could I resolve the conflict amicably and regain my sanity. It was not at all easy, but my regular practice of breathing exercises, meditation, and yoga helped me remain calm & do this.

Apply this mantra in your own life & see how it comes to your rescue too?

I understand how you may feel at times. I know very well that:

- Teenagers can be unpredictable, moody, and frustrating
- At times, parents struggle to understand & connect with them
- & You might get overwhelmed by the constant differences popping up between you & your teens
- & At the same time, confused with the various, differing suggestions from friends, family, media

But we cannot just keep on brooding on the problems. That doesn't help. We need to focus on the solutions.

And my observation in most cases is that:

- although the differences between parents and their children, especially teens, appear quite deep & difficult to bridge, yet
- actually, these differences are not that deep, &

- with the right approach, parents can strengthen their connection with their teenage son & daughter, &
- assist their teens in achieving greater heights than themselves, & then
- these well-guided teenagers, in their turn, will carry on this legacy of healthy attitude & skill to their own families, guiding their own children **(so important)**

And therefore, I ask you to apply this **"ONE TEAM"** mantra in your life. It can help you bridge your differences, resolve conflicts & become good role models for your teenager.

How to apply this mantra:

- Next time, when you fret about some misbehavior or activity of your teen, then instead of seeing your teen as the culprit, look at the issue as the culprit; for example,your teen sleeping late due to gadgets.
- Here your adversary is not your son or daughter but the gadget & its unhealthy use.
- Again, make it clear in your mind that you & your teen are one team, you both are on one side & the unhealthy gadget use is your adversary, your opponent here & together as one team you have to defeat your opponent.
- Now, when you will approach your teens with this state of mind, you will find a significant difference in your words, your tone, & your body language.

- This difference in your own state of mind has the capacity to make a significant difference in the result.
- Still some hurdles may come depending upon things like your family dynamics, your relationships with your children & other things, but without thinking too much about them here, let's take this first step first.
- Your remaining calm & centered will help you a lot in your endeavors.

And keep pursuing your goal with your team (you, your spouse & your children) on one side vs your adversaries (unhealthy gadget use in this example) on the other.

Your page

On this page note down your experience after applying the **ONE TEAM** mantra in your life.

You may also note down the hurdles you face.

Chapter 2

What keeps you awake at night??

In this chapter, let's look at the most crucial concerns about our teens so that we can pay focused attention to solving them.

In my conversations with parents in my clinic and workshops, I've come across some common concerns they have about their teenagers. I've listed these below.

Please take a look and choose the challenges that you feel are a concern to you:

- Unsatisfactory academic efforts / lack of career goals
- Excessive media usage, online gaming & related concerns
- Don't listen / don't pay attention to what you tell them
- Engaging in high-risk activities (like fast driving, not wearing helmets, or substance abuse, etc)

- Food and eating issues, including junk food, being overweight, underweight, & related concerns
- Inadequate physical activity, playing, exercising or yoga
- Poor sleep habits
- Poor respect and sense of responsibility towards parents/elders/family
- Frequent arguments - find it difficult to resolve conflicts
- Don't share their personal issues, thoughts, feelings & difficulties with you
- Mood swings and behavioral issues (like anger, aggression, feeling low, etc.)
- Infatuation / romantic relationships
- Succumbing to peer pressure / lack of self-confidence
- Reluctance to work hard / Laziness
- Poor value for money / excessive, expensive demands
- Lack of spirituality and connection to one's own culture
- Menstrual issues and hormonal imbalances (like PCOD) in girls

How are you feeling after doing the above exercise?

- Uncomfortable?
- Worried?
- Anxious?

In the next chapter, I have one personal story to share, about our son Ayam - How I overcame a difficult situation with him. That would serve as a good, practical example for you, giving hope & reassurance - **How life teaches**??

Your page

Write your main concerns regarding your son or daughter in order of your preference / importance / seriousness

Teen 1: ....

1. ____________________
2. ____________________
3. ____________________
4. ____________________
5. ____________________

Teen 2: ....

1. ____________________
2. ____________________
3. ____________________
4. ____________________
5. ____________________

Chapter 3

How life teaches??

Our son "Ayam" was born in 2004.

During the initial years, we too made some mistakes in his upbringing. But with time, maturity & new learning, we improved. We used to have a lot of good family time. And we formed a strong bond gradually.

I used to teach him mathematics. It was fun & we enjoyed it a lot, laughing & enjoying our moments together, even while studying.

He was always a brilliant student, bagging Golds & Silvers in the Olympiads.

All was well till he was in class 6th, but then it started becoming increasingly difficult to handle him.

He would hide during the time of studies & do all sorts of things, always looking to take his grandparent's mobiles to play games.

That was also the time when we had to relocate & were facing some tough challenges of our own.

We decided to go for a boarding school for him &, against all odds, he got selected in one of the top "Co-ed" boarding schools of India (Sahyadri school KFI, Pune). (There is a separate story about how we looked for a boarding school & how it all worked out).

He was there at Sahyadri School KFI from class 8-10, & excelled in various fields, including academics, sports & friendships.

And then came COVID. Classes XI & XII had to be online.

He was confused initially but finally decided to compete for Medicine as his career & joined an online coaching institute for preparing for NEET.

I had a blind faith in him & was confident that he would excel in NEET, as he had always done till then (As you will see, this blind faith cost us dearly).

And due to my blind faith, even when there were telltale signs that something is wrong, I chose to blindly trust him over Shweta (his mother) & other family members.

But what he was actually doing, he was spending almost all his time secretly playing video games during the night & sleeping during the day, hardly studying.

And when it all became apparent, it was already too late. It was a crisis. I was blamed along with Ayam& rightly so.

But, even during that turmoil, I was firm on one thing - that he can bounce back, that mistakes happen & can be rectified; that we have a strong connection & this strong connection will help him overcome it.

What Ayam witnessed then was that even when he was the one who had wronged, who had breached the trust, yet I never meant to put him down. I put the facts in front of him as such, without mincing my words, but I never meant to humiliate him.

He realized his mistake, but it was already too late.

He barely cleared his XIIth board & couldn't clear NEET for Govt. college seat in 2022.

Many of my friends & family members suggested going to a private Medical College.

Their strong argument -why risk wasting a whole year? My strong rebuttal - why risk wasting a whole life?

I was not in favor of giving my son something just like that, without him making a sufficient effort. We believed he could do better. I wanted him to have an opportunity to work out his potential, achieve on his own what best he could & redeem his self-esteem & confidence, entering the grown-up world with his head held high.

He decided to take a drop. And by that time, he only had 8 months to cover the complete syllabus for the next NEET & his not studying during his XI & XII only made the situation much more challenging for him.

We, as a family, supported him throughout (support was in many forms - empathizing, hugs, arguments, discussions, firm words, stern gestures, coercing, everything).

And in 2023, he cracked NEET. Though I still believe his potential is much more, yet given the circumstances, he did a commendable job. Right now, as I write, he is in MBBS IInd year.

I made mistakes in so many things:

- in having a blind faith on him,
- in not keeping a tab on him,
- in not heeding to my wife's warnings,
- In overlooking the telltale signs,
- in not being sufficiently firm during his XI, XII

But I was also right in so many things:

- in building a strong bonding & connection with him,
- in still having faith in him when he faltered,
- in sharing his down moments with him & not letting him feel alone,
- in not humiliating or putting him down during his weak moments

Even in the heat of the moment, I didn't forget that we are ONE TEAM. Either we both WIN or we both LOSE.

Don't assume I was soft on him. I was very firm & straightforward; I even told him that if he is not willing to work hard, he should as well be ready to take any job or do any other work. He can't just depend on what his parents have earned without putting in his own efforts.

The period was certainly very turbulent, but something helped me go through it with confidence & relative ease; my regular practices of yogic science, breathing, meditation, SKY & practical wisdom.

I was clear - YOU HAVE TO EARN IT.

And he did.

Life teaches - everyone.

And we continue to be good friends, looking forward to doing a lot of things together. Differences still arise, they ought to, but we have developed a habit of looking for solutions in place of conflicts.

What I intend to convey from my story is that mistakes happen in life in spite of our best intentions. But with sincere intentions & efforts, we can overcome them.

As I did with my son, you too might often wonder - why our otherwise intelligent teenage son or daughter commit such blunders & fail to see even the plain writing on the wall.

That is what we will talk about in the next couple of chapters - deep insights into why our teenagers act & behave the way they do? And what can we do as parents?

That will help you (as it helped me) to better understand the behaviors of your teens and respond well without losing your cool.

& Remember - as parents, it's important for you to reach out for support when you need it. It makes your life easier & helps your teenagers too.

How did you feel after reading my story?

Would you like to share some of your own life experiences? You can write to me at: admin@optimumparenting.com with the subject line: **my life experiences.**

Chapter 4

The key influencers of a teen's behavior

In the previous chapter, I shared an incident from my life, where we were left wondering, "why our otherwise intelligent teenage son or daughter act so impulsively & irrationally at times?"

As parents, you get frustrated often:

- "Why don't you listen to me?"
- "Why do you do such senseless, harmful things?"
- "इतनी simple सी चीज तुमको क्यों समझ में नहीं आती?"
- "I can't understand what gets inside you!"

Today, I'd like to share some fundamental concepts of science that will answer these questions & help you better understand & respond to your teens.

If the question is: Are the teenagers solely to be blamed for their irresponsible actions?

Then the answer is: **No, they are not.**

Then, who (or what) is responsible?

This is what we will go into now.

There are 3 key factors in a teenager's life that influence their actions & behavior:

- **Stresses / challenges** in a teenager's life
- **Their support system (Internal & External)** (or the lack of this support system)

I have discussed both the above important aspects of a teen's life in greater detail in later chapters.

For now, it's important for us to appreciate that the stresses in a teenager's life are more than what parents perceive, and that even if parents may feel - *"what's there to take so much stress about"* - for teenagers, those stresses are real & often overwhelming.

- **The way their brain is designed to work:** this is the biggest factor impacting our teen's behavior. And this is the point I want to emphasize next?

I hope you have got an idea about the key factors influencing your teen's actions & behavior.

As you begin to appreciate & address these factors, it will begin to make a significant difference in your teenager's as well as your own lives. But, first we will have to understand clearly about how a teen brain functions.

"Is it their fault if their brain is designed to work in a certain way?" is what we will look at.

Only after looking at this puzzle from all angles, will we be able to solve it.

This is what the next chapter brings for you.

Chapter 5

The Accelerator & the Brake

We briefly talked about the key factors influencing a teenager's actions in the previous chapter.

One of them - the way their brain is designed to work - is very crucial for every parent to understand. Let's do that.

To put it simply, let's say there are two parts of the brain:

- Part 1 is the **"Accelerator system"** - the impulsive, emotional and thrill-seeking part of the brain; &
- Part 2 is the **"Brake system"** - the controlling & regulating part, which protects us from taking dangerous actions & decisions.
- While the "Accelerator system" is already well developed and powerful during teenage years,
- the "Brake system" is still developing and takes time to mature (it typically matures around 23-25 years of age)

- So, most young people are impulsive until around 23-25 years of age, and maturity to control their impulsive actions comes only gradually.

This imbalance in brain development makes it difficult for teenagers to resist temptations. Even when they are well aware of the dangers. they just act as puppets in the hands of their emotions & perceived compulsions, rather than going by logic or rationality.

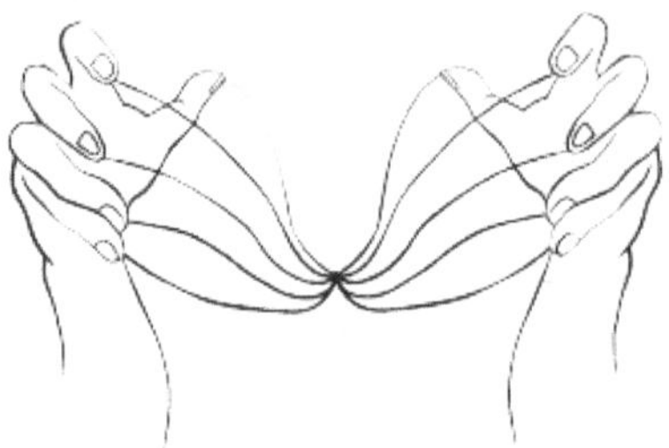

That's why, even when they are aware of & understand about the harms of things like:

- Smoking / Drugs / alcohol
- Unhealthy media use
- Not studying well
- Not sleeping on time
- Not eating right
- Not exercising
- Careless driving / dangerous stunts

They still find it difficult to resist themselves from indulging in these activities or doing course correction.

At times, they are the ones to give in to the pressure of their peer group & at other times they become the ones exerting pressure over their peers.

Powerful Accelerators, Poor Brakes - Results are not difficult to imagine.

It's not their fault per se; it's how their brain is designed to work. And therefore we, parents, have to play the role of brakes in the accelerated lives of our teenagers. (But, is that easy?)

Question: Why should you know this?

Answer: Because, when you know and appreciate this:

- You won't always see your teens as the culprit
- The blame game towards them inside your mind would decrease
- You would become more patient and understanding
- Your acceptance of their apparent wrong behavior would improve
- And this will help you stay emotionally connected to them, even during difficult times, & get the right response needed to support & protect them. (like applying the "one team" mantra).

And this is so important, you see. Your whole approach may just shift to a more positive one after this understanding. Remember, being grown-ups, our brake system ought to be more mature by now & therefore our response has to be more mature.

And then, here is another very, very important thing you should know & keep in mind. The following factors can further delay the development of the brain's control or the brake system in teens:

- wrong food
- poor sleep / rest
- inadequate physical activity
- unhealthy media usage
- chronic stress / feeling of insecurity / lack of adequate support
- substance abuse - smoking, alcohol, drugs, etc
- environmental pollution

Please check how many of the above factors are working to delay maturity in the case of your own son or daughter? Because, if there are, you need to do something about them as soon as you can. Consider it nothing less than an emergency.

Otherwise, it becomes a vicious cycle where one negative factor amplifies another, creating a chain reaction of harmful consequences.

Oh-oh-oh, I can almost hear you lamenting, "But what do I do, he/she doesn't listen to me".

That's right, how would you, if they don't listen? To be able to influence the critical aspects of your teenager's life, they ought to listen to you & for that, you ought to have some rapport with them. Or else, the advice would fall on deaf ears.

And this brings us to the most important aspect of parenting a teenager, which I'll talk about next.

IMPORTANT!

If you have to work on just one thing & correct only one thing with respect to your teenage son or daughter, this is it.

Oh, & do I hear another loud question inside you, "but this fact of science must also have been there when we were teens, but we were not so arrogant. Then, what has changed now?"

Here I share an inscription from a 6000-year-old Egyptian tomb:

We live in a decaying age. Young people no longer respect their parents. They are rude and impatient. They frequently inhabit taverns and have no self-control.

You see, these issues have always been there since when - since 6000 years or even more, who knows!!

So, ask yourself: What has changed now from when you yourself were a teenager? - Finding the answer to this is your homework.

In the next chapter I will share another real-life story, of one of my patients. Again, a story which gives us hope & comfort.

Your pages

- Please choose how many of these are significant in the case of your own son / daughter? & what can you do about them?
- Wrong food
- Poor sleep
- Inadequate physical activity
- Unhealthy media usage
- Chronic stress
- Feeling of insecurity / lack of adequate support
- Substance abuse - smoking, alcohol, drugs, etc
- Environmental pollution

- What has changed now from when you yourself were a teen?

Chapter 6

A happy beginning

Today, I will tell you a story - a happy ending story.

Once upon a time, not so long ago, in a bustling city, not so far away, in a small sweet home, lived a young, loving couple - Jatin and Anika.

They were blessed with a charming little boy - Vihan.

They were a happy family, always laughing, playing, and learning together.

Vihan was a curious little boy who loved to explore the world around him with his parents as his protectors.

As a young boy, Vihan eagerly listened to Jatin and Anika's every word.

They would ask him to do something, and he would run to do it. They would tell him not to do something, and he would stop right away. He was a perfect little angel.

Jatin and Anika would beam with pride, knowing they were raising a well-mannered and obedient child.

They had almost complete control over Vihan's life & decisions.

Vihan would want to be involved in everything his parents were doing:

- If they were working in the kitchen, he would come there.
- If they were doing some office work, he would barge in.
- If they were having a meeting or a party, he would want to be there too.

At times, Jatin & Anika would get irritated, angry, and might even shout - "Hey, this is not your job, don't irritate me; you'll only spoil everything; go play, do something of your own".

Time flew by, and Vihan was around six or maybe seven at that time. He started to ignore his parents' instructions & even question them. He would do things if he felt like it, and wouldn't if he didn't.

Jatin and Anika noticed the change, but they thought it was just a passing phase.

As Vihan approached his pre-teens, his attitude towards his parents shifted even more. Now, he would even shout back.

"Is this what we have taught you?" Jatin and Anika would lament.

Now Vihan entered his teenage years & the once-close family seemed to be drifting further away.

The intimate connection they once shared seemed like vanishing, replaced by a constant "Cold War."

Jatin and Anika felt heartbroken.

They couldn't understand why their once-loving son was now so distant.

Sometimes they felt like they had failed as parents.

Pause .....

The same children who, when they were kids, wanted to be involved in everything you did and followed almost all of your instructions, now show less interest in being involved with you and don't listen to you as they grow.

I have some questions for you today:

- Have you seen this type of story happening around you?
- Why does it happen?
- Guess & then Google how many times a young child gets to hear the word "NO" in one day?
- What is the meaning of the words - Negative Communication, Positive communication & Quality time?

Ponder about these questions & write in your diary, before you go on to read the next chapter.

Honest answers to these questions have the power to lead you to the root cause of a number of your issues & help you in finding your solutions.

Remember, taking the right action is the key to getting the right results. The story will conclude in the next chapter with a happy ending.

See you there.

Your pages

- How many times a young child gets to hear the word "NO" or gets exposed to negative communication in one day?
  - Your own Guess....................................?
  - What does Google say..................................?

- Your ideas about - Negative Communication

- Your ideas about - Positive communication

- Your ideas about - Quality time

Chapter 7

A happy ending

The story continues ...

Though Jatin & Anika believed that there was no major fault on their part, yet they decided to sit down and reflect.

They discussed within themselves, took help & spent time in introspection

They realized that Vihan's growing independence & indifference might be a natural part of growing up which they had failed to notice or probably overlooked.

They realized that they needed to adjust their approach to better support and guide their teenage son & be a real support to him, rather than seeking complete control over his life decisions & taking him for granted.

With this newfound understanding, they decided to spend more quality time with Vihan.

One day, when Vihan returned home from school, he found a family photo album on the living room table.

He started flipping through the pages, and memories of forgotten happier times came flooding back - parents holding him as a baby with warmth in their eyes and joy on their faces; a family vacation at the beach, building sandcastles together, jumping through the waves, laughter all around; blowing out the candles on the birthday cake.

With each page turned, Vihan's heart swelled with love for the beautiful moments they had shared.

It was then that Jatin and Anika joined him, hugged him tight, and they all began reminiscing about the past.

Jatin and Anika took this opportunity to share with Vihan how much they loved him and how they missed the closeness they once had.

They acknowledged that at times, they might have been, knowingly or unknowingly, rude to him & said sorry for those times.

They acknowledged that they needed to give Vihan more freedom to grow and learn, while still being there for him at every juncture of his life, to support him.

They said they never meant to hurt their loving son.

Vihan, while hugging back tightly, was trying hard to stop his flowing tears.

As the days went by, Jatin, Anika, and Vihan started to reconnect.

They shared their thoughts, feelings, and dreams with one another.

They started doing activities together again, like going for a walk, watching movies together, and discussing future goals.

And so, the family of Jatin, Anika, and Vihan slowly rebuilt their relationship.

It was not easy & required the right approach, patience & regular handholding for the parents too.

They learned to respect each other's opinions, communicate openly, and cherish the time they spent together.

Through love, patience and understanding, they faced the challenges of Vihan's teenage years and emerged as a stronger, more united family.

The story ends happily.

After reading the story, are some thoughts coming to your mind?

You may write in your diary what you are thinking or feeling.

I earnestly wish all families are so lucky.

And that's what I aim at in all my interactions with teenagers & parents, in all my programs & workshops for parents & teens.

At this point in our book, I have some intense action steps for you, which I will give you in the next chapter.

ARE YOU READY?

Chapter 8

Reversing the wheel of Hurt

Your child has now grown up and is no longer the little kid he or she once was:

- & there has been quite a lot of struggle between you
- & if you think you made some bad, hurting mistakes when they were younger.
- & regret those moments
- & want to reverse the hurt & their consequences
- & wonder if anything can be done now

Then, this message is for you.

Yes, a lot can be done.

First, let go of any guilt you might be harboring. It happens to everyone. Whatever a parent does is only with the best intention for their child.

Second, make a list of the mistakes you believe you've made, without covering them up or thinking of any excuses.

(It's important to note that the child's reactions or mistakes are not the focus here. Your children must surely have made a lot of mistakes, spoken back, been rude, etc, but here, our attention is solely on the parent's actions and thoughts).

So, you now have a list of mistakes that you have made, knowingly or unknowingly, which may have hurt your child & impacted your relations adversely. (You don't need to show this list to your child; it's just for you)

Make a note of the most important 3-5 of this list of mistakes.

Then, with an open heart, go to your child, hold his/her hand and say, "Son/daughter/friend, I need to talk to you about something important".

Your pure intention, the tone of this one sentence, which has love, affection, a sense of responsibility, regret for the wrong, and a longing to correct it – this one sentence will breach your child's resistance & reach their heart.

Children (of all ages) just want love from their parents, love & support, some respect, some guidance and less judgment.

Just say, "I (or we) feel that I've made some mistakes, and I want to share them with you," and then say them out; and.....Done.

If you remember any particular incidents, share them too.

Then, lovingly stroke their head or hug them (or whatever physical touch you are comfortable with) for as long as you can.

And seeing them eye to eye, sincerely say, "I am SORRY" (while still holding them)

Parents, we are more mature & hence we have to take the first steps, keeping our ego aside.

Remember – **ONE TEAM**

Please take these steps today, and after doing them - write in your diary, how you felt & what happened.

Your page

On this page note down your experience after applying the steps for reversing the wheel of hurt & the hurdles you faced

Chapter 9

Do you really love your Child??

I hope you have completed your assignment from the previous chapter.

Now here I have a question for you - Do you love your children?

Isn't that a silly question?

Nonetheless, it's a very pertinent silly question.

Tell me, when you love someone/something, what do you do?

For example, if you love badminton, or books, or shopping, or movies, what do you do?

Yes... you spend more and more quality time with them.

So, how much **Quality Time** do you spend with your children, young & grownups? And what do you do during that time?

If there's ONE THING a parent should work on, before anything else, it is - strengthening your bond & connection with your children, spending quality time with them.

You may ask: "How do I spend quality time with my teenage children? We don't have much in common now."

I would say:

- Keep it simple
- Be honest
- Share your life with them & let them share theirs
- Talk, listen - without judgments, prejudices or premonitions
- Give your children the freedom to say what they want to say, even if you disagree (A question for you here: how comfortable do you think your teenagers feel voicing their disagreements with you?)
- Offer support and guidance while respecting their growing independence
- Stay updated; don't look down on every new trend
- Accept the differences; & then strive to discard your discomfort with the differences
- Stay as fit & as sharp as possible - If you want the respect and friendship of young children, it helps to be fit, sharp & have a great sense of humor.

And while still being a parent, strive to become their friend too.

Who is a friend? - Someone who thinks at your level, understands your feelings, your difficulties, sees the world through your eyes, one you can talk to openly without hesitation, is always ready to help without making you feel small & doesn't judge you all the time.

So, if you become their friend, your children will start to open up to you, and the differences between you will start to decrease.

And when the differences decrease, better communication starts.

And when better communication starts, better solutions happen.

Without effective communication, how would you be able to guide them?

Remember, Quality Time isn't just about when you are directly interacting with your teen. The moments in between those direct interactions, your body language throughout the day, the tone of your voice, especially when they have made some mistakes, these and hundreds of such small things all play a crucial role.

As homework, I ask for two things from you, the reader parent:

- Reflect on the thought patterns and feelings deep inside of you about your teenage son or daughter. Become aware of all the pride or dissatisfaction you harbor for them; & then
- Write them down in two lists: one list for the things that make you proud of them and another for any grievances & complaints you might be harboring towards them.

This self-awareness will further help you approach them with more understanding and empathy.

Your pages

Your inner feelings about your teenage son & daughter:

- What you feel proud of:

1. ______
2. ______
3. ______
4. ______
5. ______

______

- Your grievances & complaints:

1. ______
2. ______
3. ______
4. ______
5. ______

______

______

Chapter 10

What's stopping you??

Did you complete the homework from the last chapter?

I hope you did.

Now, look at these situations:

- watching TV/movies sitting together with your children but without deeper interaction
- having dinner together but with everyone focused on their phones
- talking to them about their studies, sports or other fields & focusing only on their results, without actually listening to the difficulties they are facing
- celebrating their birthday, but not focusing on what they would enjoy the most
- taking family trips, visiting relatives or attending family events without having meaningful conversations with your teenager

- being absorbed in your screens or in taking selfies during picnics, rather than enjoying the moments
- doing any activity together but not paying sufficient attention to their feelings, thoughts, experiences or point of view; their likes, dislikes and whether they are enjoying that activity or not

❖ Can any of the mentioned situations be considered as quality time?

❖ &, would these increase the bonding or the distance?

There are a lot of such situations in your daily life where you get the opportunity to strengthen your connection with your children.

And every parent can & should use these moments to connect with them.

It's not only for the children; you yourself will be healed from within.

Please note: Teenagers need a trusted, connected adult in their life to prevent them from risk-taking behavior & resisting a lot of other negative influences, temptations, & peer pressure in their life.

- When they receive enough love and support from their parents, they become more confident and resilient enough to resist the influence of these negative environmental factors.
- However, when they fail to get this love & support from their parents or caretakers, the same temptations can overpower & influence your child.

So, as parents, it's crucial to have a strong connection with your teenage children. This not only helps them during their teenage years but also creates a strong foundation for a lifelong relationship, bringing joy and strength to all of you.

But I come across many parents who struggle to become friends with their teenagers.

- Why is that?
- What's stopping you & what can you do?

That's what we will be looking at in the next lesson.

Your page

Do you struggle to become friends with your teenager?

- If yes, why?
- What's stopping you?
- What can you do?

Chapter 11

Authority, Discipline & a mind-blowing Idea

As we were talking in the last chapter, many parents find it difficult to connect & become friends with their teenage children. Let's see why:

- **Generational differences:** not having much in common with the teens.
- **Communication challenges:**
- **Busy schedule of both - parents and teens**

Don't worry; quality time is less about the number of hours.

It's more about the quality in the available number of hours. And this is most certainly not so difficult to improve. Be watchful of your inner feelings towards your teen. Are the feelings more of discontent & complaints or are you equally proud of their qualities, talents & achievements? The exercises for you after Chapter 9 would have helped you improve this awareness.

- **Fear of losing authority:** yes, this might be a genuine concern, that becoming too friendly with your teen might result in loss of your authority over them & a balance is required. Because you may feel that without sufficient authority, you won't be able to guide & prevent them from harm. And that's a genuine concern.

But, where does this authority come from? Do you remember the following sentence from Ch 9?

And while still being a parent, strive to become their friend too.

A parent has to maintain their place & respect, but can't that be done in friendlier manner, in a more dignified way?

It can be done & it has to be done.

Please understand that you can have real respect & authority over your children only when:

- you spend sufficient quality time with them,
- there is a deep connection between you,
- they respect you in spite of your differences.

REMEMBER

- **Love = Quality time & Connection**
- **Quality time & Connection = Authority**
- **Authority = Discipline**

As a parent, your aim has to be to strike a balance between maintaining a strong connection/friendship and preserving your respect & authority. In today's world, a parent can't claim authority over their children just by default. They will have to earn it.

And if, for any reason, you find it difficult, you should strive to learn & nurture this critical parenting skill.

Because it's crucial in today's world to have this skill.

However, even after all this, if, for some reason (like past prejudices, premonitions & conflicts), you are not able to bridge your communication gap with your teenager & find it difficult to make friends with them, I have a way out, one easier solution for you. It has worked for many parents & there is no reason why it should not work for you.

The mind-blowing easy solution is:

Become friends with their friends.

In contrast to your own teens, you might find it way easier to connect with their friends because there is little or no baggage of preconceptions, expectations, or prior conflicts.

And then, when your teen hears their friends say, "Yaar, your mom is so cool, your dad is so cool", it opens up a new window for you to build a stronger connection with your own teen.

Give it a try and see the difference it can create in your relationship with your teenager.

But, remember one thing - all your endeavors have to come from a space of genuine openness & love & not from a space of intent to manipulate.

I hope you get what I mean. Our relationships have to be based on honest intentions & sincerity, to be able to give us that fulfillment in our life which they are meant for.

Chapter 12

Teenagers want to listen to you! But they don't - why?

As a pediatrician and an adolescent + parent guide, I've met hundreds of parents who find it hard to talk, share their feelings, and convey their messages to their kids, especially teenagers.

Parents say - Children don't listen
Teenagers say - Parents don't understand

But it's so important. As we discussed in a previous chapter also, "A trusted adult guidance is very important for a teenager".

So, what should you do?

Because, without being on the same page, how would you, as parents, be able to help your teens and protect them from negative influences?

Let me tell you what I have discovered from my innumerable encounters with children & teens:

- They have so many confusions in life about which they want guidance. They want to listen to a trusted adult.

- **And deep down they want that trusted adult to be their "mummy & papa".**
- Parents just need to know why they don't & how they will.

So, let's first see why they don't want to listen.

Many parents genuinely believe that the friction is entirely the child's fault. It never occurs to them that they might also be or even more responsible for the friction & communication gap. They think they have all the knowledge & experience & understanding of how things work in the world, while their teenagers don't know much. With this biased belief, their communication gets biased too & hence fails to connect.

(Please read these lines a few more times & let them sink in well)
On the backdrop of the above understanding, let's now see some of the main reasons why kids, as they grow, stop listening to & sharing with their parents.

1. Constant Lecturing:

As children grow, the topics change but the lecturing continues:

- "You're so lazy; your room is always a mess"
- "You never care about your studies; God knows what will become of you"
- "Why can't you dress like a normal, sane person?"

- "Your friends are such losers; why can't you find some sensible ones?"
- "All the time you're on your phone. No wonder you don't do anything else."
- & so on

Result: Teenagers become annoyed & don't want to talk or listen

2. Not (sufficiently) respecting their feelings:

For example, if they're upset about a friend's behavior, in place of empathizing with them, parents may say:

- What's such a big deal about it?
- Why are you so upset about it?
- It's such a small thing. Why are you creating so much fuss?
- Come on, get over it quickly

Result: Teenagers feel not heard, not supported or cared enough & don't feel like sharing their feelings in future

3. **Lack of trust & confidence:** even on small matters

- You'll cook dinner? You can't even toast the bread without burning it.
- Drive? No way, you'll crash the car.
- You chose that subject? Seriously? You really think you can handle it

Result: Teenagers lose faith in their own abilities; their self-confidence & self-esteem take a blow.

4. **Inconsistency in rules:**

- One day, you let your child stay up late watching TV, but the next day, you scold them for the same.
- One week you don't say anything about your teenager's messy room, but the next week, you suddenly become furious about the same.

Result: Teenagers get confused

5. **Not leading by example (not walking the talk):**

- You tell your teenager to avoid spending too much time on their phone, but you yourself are constantly scrolling through social media or playing games on your device.
- You expect your child to always be on time but you yourself are seldom on time.

Result: Teenagers feel unfair & you lose their respect, especially if this happens frequently.

6. **And then there are other factors like:**

- Just trying to impose what parents feel to be right without paying attention to their teenager's point of view or feelings;
- Interrupting the teens while they're expressing their views;
- Not spending enough quality time together

I have a question for you here: If someone behaved towards you in the manner described above, what would you do?

- Avoid them
- Look forward to talking & sharing with them

Did you choose your response? - Thank you for your patience & your understanding.

And please note that, in today's era, respect is mutual & has to be earned. Just because you are a parent or a teacher doesn't mean that you will be respected by today's teens irrespective of how you behave. You will have to earn their respect by your actions & then respect them too. If you don't respect the feelings of your teens, chances are they

also won't respect yours.

We had quite a lot of discussion on communication challenges.

But, only focusing on problems doesn't solve anything.

So, let's come to the solution.

- This is what we will look at in the next chapters.
- Tips which will make it easier for you to communicate with your teens

Chapter 13

Your teens will open up

We already talked about the importance of:

- Saying sorry for our mistakes, &
- Spending quality time with our children

All parents ought to remember that these are the first & the most important two things for us apply to develop deep bonding with & to open up our teens.

Now, let's see what more we can do to make our daily communication better & more connecting.

One thing is undisputed - Whatever parents may say or do, they only want the best for their children, even if it might hurt the kid's feelings at times.

So, can we, as parents, convey the same message, voice our concerns, but in a nicer, non-hurting language? Let's look at the same examples from the previous chapters to see how we can do this.

Voicing the same concerns in a more positive tone:

- Instead of: "You're so lazy; your room is always a mess"
- **Try saying:** "I often find your room untidy. Do you need my help to clean it? It will make both of us feel better & you might also feel more organized & decluttered."
- Instead of: "You never care about your studies; God knows what will become of you"
- **Try saying:** "I feel that you are not paying sufficient attention to your studies. Is it so? & Can we talk about what's going on or if something's troubling you?"
- Instead of: "Drive? No way, you'll crash the car like last time"
- **Try saying**: "Yes, you ought to drive now. Remember, we had a close call last time. Let's practice a bit more before you go alone"
- Instead of: "Your friends are such losers; why can't you find some sensible ones?"
- **Try saying:** "I'm concerned about your friends. My judgment may be wrong, but I feel worried & we need to discuss it."
- Instead of: "Full-time you're on your phone. No wonder you can't focus on anything else."

- **Try saying:** "I feel you spend a lot of time on your phone. Isn't that so? Do you think that's good for you? What can we do about it?"
- Instead of: "Cook dinner? You can't even make toast without burning it."
- **Try saying**: "Great that you want to cook dinner tonight? Please serve less burned toast this time (teasing & laughing)"
- Instead of: "Why can't you dress like a normal, sane person?"
- **Try saying:** "Your dressing style makes me uncomfortable. We need to talk about it."
- Instead of: "You chose that subject? Seriously? You really think you can handle it"
- **Try saying**: "This subject you're choosing looks quite challenging. Are you sure you've thought it through? I think we should consult a professional before taking the final call"

These expressions convey the same concerns, but in a more supportive & nonjudgmental way. They help children to open up to you rather than cutting off further communication.

I hope the point is clear for you to understand & practice.

The homework for you is to practice this change in voicing your concerns.

Although I would like to emphasize here that more than what words you are using, the tone, the space of concern from which you are talking, & your intention are much more important. Pay attention on these along with your choice of words & see the wonder unfolding before you.

Your page

Could you rephrase your words as discussed in this chapter?

- What was your experience?
- What hurdles did you face?

Chapter 14

Talk & connect with one super helpful idea

We continue from the previous chapter.

There are more little things, small changes you can do, to make a big difference.

Let's look at one such super helpful tip. These three, when applied together, can greatly improve communication with your teenager:

- asking open questions,
- listening carefully, &
- acknowledging / respecting their feelings

Imagine a usual conversation:

- You: "How was your day?"
- Daughter: "Fine"
- You: "What did you do?"
- Daughter: "Nothing"

End of conversation.

Open questions mean questions which can't easily be answered with a single word or just a "yes" or "no". These help the teens to say more & open up. Such questions convey that you are more deeply concerned about their lives.

Let's look at some examples for a better understanding of what it means:

Example 1: Your teen comes home looking stressed

- Instead of asking "Did you have a bad day?" (which can be answered with a simple "yes" or "no")
- Try asking, "You seem upset. What happened?" with concern, pausing whatever you were doing to listen (& maybe also holding their hands)

This encourages them to share more details and gives you a chance to provide support.

Example 2: Your teen is upset because they didn't get invited to a friend's party.

- Instead of dismissing their feelings by saying, "It's just a party"
- Acknowledge their emotions & say: "I understand you must be feeling very upset & left out. Do you have any idea why you were not invited?"

Further communication depends on their response.

Please keep in mind:

- ➢ The way you word your conversation is just one aspect.
- ➢ More importantly, the space of mind from which you come, the concerns, empathy and respect you have for

your teen influences your body language and the tone of your voice, which are crucial in deciding their response.

Please pay attention to both the above points.

Example 3: Your teenager is struggling with a decision about whether to join a sports team or an art club.

- Rather than saying, "both are useless" or saying "choose anyone, doesn't make a difference"
- You empathize with their confusion and help them by discussing the pros and cons of each as per the likes & personality of your child. This way, they feel understood in their concerns & supported in their decisions.

And some other crucial pointers:

- Generously & genuinely praise & appreciate your child
- Yet, you don't have to be goody-goody all the time
- **Criticize firmly when required without fearing their backlash**
- But no need to be rude while criticizing or saying "No"
- It's possible to "say No with a smile"
- **How you say things matters more to teens than what you're saying or what is right or wrong; so please be aware of the tone of your voice**
- Remember to criticize in person & appreciate in public

- Remember, it's normal for teens to be moody
- Don't worry if they seem to like their friends more than you. That's just how teenagers are.

And remember, while talking with them:

- **Put your phone down** / turn off the TV
- Sit down with them
- See eye to eye / (maybe hold hands) and
- Listen intently without interrupting

Showing understanding and support, without judging or criticizing them for having a different perspective or opinion, creates a comfortable space for them to speak their minds.

Open communication is the key to a strong bond. Every teenager wants to feel comfortable with their parents, having this confidence that they'll be heard, understood, supported and guided wherever needed.

By regularly practicing open communication + attentive listening + respecting their feelings, your teen will start to trust you more and feel comfortable sharing even their deepest concerns with you.

How valuable do you think this trust is?

- Always remember, even if they don't say it, they really need you; & need you more now than when they were younger
- Deep inside, they're craving words of love, appreciation, approval & guidance from you

And as we conclude the topic of communication, here is a modern trick which I have used with superb results & you can too.

The trick is:

Using your mobile phones for communication:

- If there is something you feel is difficult to say face to face, use WhatsApp or any other media. There you can also phrase & rephrase your words carefully, unlike spoken words.
- You & your teens must be there in different family groups on WhatsApp or other media. You can put a message or a funny meme or forward some post about what you want to convey to your teens in that group. That conveys the message without you being the one saying those directly.
- We have created a common WA group of Ayam & his close circle of MBBS friends with the name "Family Zone". There we put messages & memes like the importance of sleep, the right food, the harm of smoking & many other things. This also gives him courage to face undue peer pressure.
- By such communication, you can convey your thoughts & there is no direct confrontation either. Also, it is fun & hence a strong message goes into their subconscious mind.
- In the next chapter, we will talk about what to do when even the most empathetic words fail.

Your pages

Communicate the way as discussed in this chapter?

- What was your experience?
- What hurdles did you face?

Chapter 15

Jadu ki Jhappi

You know, there's something magical about the power of touch, especially for children.

Remember when they were little and a simple hug was the universal medicine - a fall, a terrifying dream, a lost toy - a tight hug, a comforting embrace & all was solved.

Now, as they've grown into teenagers, they may act like they don't care about your hugs or touch anymore. But don't get fooled by this grown-up facade of theirs.

Your touch still has the same magic, and they need it just as much if not more than they did when they were little.

In previous chapters, we discussed how to talk so they listen.

But there's more to communication than just words.

A simple touch has the power to convey more than the best-chosen words.

When words fail or arguments heat up, a gentle touch can say what words can't.

It says:

- I'm here for you
- I understand
- I care no matter what

It builds a strong bridge between you and your teen.

Think about it. When your teenager is stressed about a test, upset over a conflict with a friend, frustrated with you or even themselves, a hug or even a simple touch can provide so much comfort.

It's a sincere, silent way of saying, "I'm here for you, and we'll get through this together."

On the other hand, when they do well in their exams, get selected in a team, or just make a right decision, a high-five, a pat on the back, or even a “thumbs up” can make them feel so good. Again, it's a silent "Well done. I'm so proud of you."

Just like we learned to use a more positive voice, we can also use a more positive touch to shower our love and support.

It's a small thing which makes a big difference.

Give it a try, and you might be surprised at the results.

Yet, I have seen many Indian parents shying away from physical touch, especially hugging, once their children have grown up.

Are you one of them?

If so, you're missing out (& your teens too) on something really powerful. So, let go of your hesitation & make the best use of this magic, this जादू की झप्पी (Jadu ki jhappi).

You might not know it, but you yourself are craving this power of touch. Physical touch will not only comfort your children but also heal you from within.

And I also see many teenagers feeling shy over public displays of affection from their parents. In that case, don't embarrass them with a big hug in front of others. Save those moments for the quiet of your home. That's your personal "us" time.

So, that's the homework from this chapter. Hug your son & daughter & say a few nice things to them.

Do it now; & then make it a habit.

Your page

Did you give a tight hug to your son & daughter?

- Yes
- No

- What happened after that?
- Anything else you would like to express, please write here.

Chapter 16

Stresses in a teen's life are real

It's important for parents to realize that the stresses in a typical teenager's life today are often much more than what the parents think.

And even though the parents might feel that their worries aren't that big, for teenagers, these worries are very real & big.

What are these stresses? Let's look at the main reasons for stress in the life of a teenager:

- **Lots of sudden changes in their body & mind:** Their bodies are changing, their thoughts are changing, feelings are changing, and the changes are rapid. Not all teens may be ready for these sudden changes, causing confusion & stress.
- **Confusing expectations from adults around them:** At times we adults expect them to just listen to us (because in our opinion they are still immature) & at other times we expect them to behave like adults

(because, in our opinion, now they have grown up). You see, we adults are ourselves confused about how we expect them to act, only adding to their confusion & stress.

- **Peer pressure and the urgent need to fit in:** is a major source of stress for most teenagers. They often feel pressured to behave in certain ways or to adopt certain styles or wear certain clothes or listen to certain music or indulge in certain activities to be accepted by their peer groups. This constant urge to fit in & being approved creates a lot of stress. Research shows that peer pressure can increase risk-taking behavior by about 50% in vulnerable children.

- **Bullying:** whether it happens in real life or on the internet, can really mess with the minds of young, vulnerable teens.

- **Conflicts in friendship and relationships:** when there's a conflict with a friend (boy or girl), it can feel like the end of the world to a teen. Conflicts with parents are another big source of stress.

- **School & academic Pressure:** studies, homework, tests, exams, competitive exams, time management.

- **Career confusions:** for example, undue emphasis on certain traditional fields, like engineering or medicine, without paying attention to their likes & dislikes, strengths & weaknesses.

- **Social media & digital world:** can cause comparisons, inferiority complex, depression, anxiety, low self-esteem, poor time management, sleep deprivation, cyberbullying & more.

- **Body Image (and related self-esteem) Issues:** This is the age when teens become more conscious of their physical appearance, leading to stress due to how they feel they look, which is often amplified by the media and social media.

- **Doubts about sex, their sexual orientation** (meaning who they're attracted to), pregnancy, contraception & other such queries: during their teenage years, they are figuring out who they are. Parents often dismiss these as trivial issues or become uncomfortable talking about these, but teens get a lot of stress due to all these questions & lack of guidance. This big elephant has been sitting in the room for a long, long time & needs to be addressed without any further delay.

It's important to remember that every teenager may experience different stresses to different degrees, or have additional stressors not listed here. But, every teen has stress in their lives. And as we discussed already, parents ought to listen with attention & acknowledge their feelings.

When I talk about these things with parents:

- Some of them say, "Oh, we never realized my son or daughter would be going through so much. But then, what do we do?"

- & some say, "Why so much fuss about it? Everybody has to face stress in life. I don't want my children to

> be weak & become dependent on me for every little thing. They ought to be strong & handle their issues by themselves now. These stresses would make them bold & tough. Let them face it."

The question is, how we, as parents, can help our teenagers to face these stresses & emerge out bolder, tougher & stronger.

Let's see.

Chapter 17

Stresses in your teen's life - some Do's & Don'ts for you

Yes, stress in life is inevitable -for everyone? And everyone ought to learn to handle them.

And do you now realize it might be inevitable & real for your teen too? As we discussed in the previous chapter; and that you need to do something about it.

You see, some short-term stress is acceptable, whether for adults or children.

The real problem comes when:

- stress persists for long, or
- we don't do anything about it, &
- the teens are left alone, unsupported & to fend for themselves without adequate guidance or support

Here's the thing - when teenagers are feeling stressed, they might try to talk to their parents about it.

When parents:

- understand & empathize with their children
- support them, &
- help them address the core issue

The stress is short-lived & doesn't cause many problems.

But if the parents say:

- Don't take stress
- What's there to feel so stressed about?
- Why are you being so weak?
- How come you fret so much about such small things?
- Why don't you behave like a grown up?
- This is nothing. You'll know real stress when you grow up

What do you think, would it help?

- just saying "don't take stress" doesn't work. Right!
- can you manage your stress just by saying so?
- then, how can we expect our children to?

So, when parents brush off their teens' worries just like that & try to make them feel like their issues aren't a big deal, or the teens are left on their own to sort their way out, the stress tends to persist for a longer time. And the issue may even remain unresolved.

This longer-lasting, 'chronic', or unresolved stress has:

- really, really serious effects
- short term as well as long term
- physical, mental as well as psychological

This approach of leaving a teen unsupported & alone to fight for themselves even during the initial stages of teenage is unlikely to make them strong. It's like expecting a small, fragile plant to thrive by itself without providing sufficient support even in the beginning when they are weak & need the support. It's more likely to weaken them further & instill fear in their minds. To begin with, you have to support them in their initial struggles & gradually as they become stronger & more capable, let them handle their challenges on their own.

- The point I'm trying to make is that, just as a plant requires initial, adequate support and nourishment to grow strong, so does a teenager, especially in the face of so many challenges, especially in the early stages of their teenage years.
- It's only after receiving this support that they can be expected to emerge strong to navigate life's challenges independently.

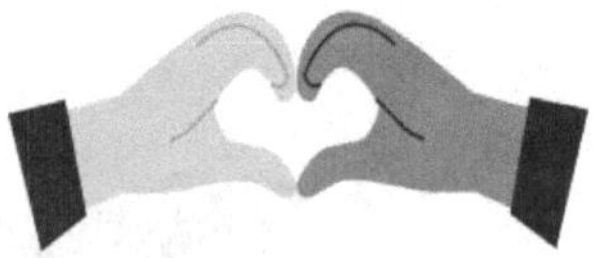

Now, if you have developed good communication with your teenager, they will approach & directly talk to you when they're feeling stressed. And you will be able to provide support.

However, if:

- Your communication is not so open yet
- or when sometimes they themselves don't realize they're stressed (yes, this also happens with all of us)
- or there is some such issue which they are not comfortable or confident in sharing with you

Then, in such situations, their stress may show in various different ways which are unexplained medically & often baffle a parent.

These are the most common expressions of stress in teenagers in such situations:

- recurrent unexplained headaches
- recurrent unexplained abdominal pain
- other pains like backache, pain in muscles or soft parts of the body
- increased or decreased sleep
- increased or decreased appetite &/or weight
- not feeling well

- not feeling like doing anything
- etc

Why is this important for a parent to know? Well, if your teenager is displaying any symptoms that don't have a clear explanation, stress might be the cause. And when you recognize that, you will be able to address it or share your concern with your doctor & resolve it.

In the next chapters, we will discuss a very vital aspect of your teen's lives. How can they overcome these stresses successfully?

- their external support system
- their internal support system

Chapter 18

Teen's External Support System

So, there are two things:.

- challenges in life, &
- the support system to overcome these challenges

Facing challenges and dealing with stress becomes easier when one has a stronger support system. A strong support system not only acknowledges and understands our feelings but also provides us with the much-needed strength during our weak moments.

But, my observation over the last few years has been that, while the challenges in the life of a teenager are increasing day by day, their support system is falling short & is inadequate.

Have you also felt like this at times?

As per a WHO study, 40-45% of teenagers in India are facing some or other behavioral/mental issues. And this figure is increasing day by day. Most issues begin as behavioral ones, & when not addressed in time, or adequately enough, tend to aggravate into more problematic mental and psychiatric issues.

The data also says that only 5-10% have access to some type of professional help, and even when it's available, teenagers seldom want to take it unless their friends tell them to. That's another very important reason why parents also need to become friends with their teenagers.

Let's look into who all form the external support system for a teenager in their lives:

1. Family:

The family, and especially the parents (should), form the first, immediate & the most vital support system for their teen.

As parents, your role is most important & you should be the first one they think of reaching out to when going through a tough time.

Q for you: Whom do your teens reach out to first, when stressed?

& Why?

(Have you ever thought about this)

2. Friends:

Next come the friends - mutual pillars of strong, unconditional support for each other.

Friends form an important second line of support & in many cases the first line.

However, if a teen can't talk openly to their parents, friends become their only option.

And since these friends themselves might be facing similar issues, will they be able to give the most mature or objective advice? (नीम हकीम खतरा-ए-जान)

And then, in today's era, there are online and offline predators, lurking in the garb of friends, waiting to take advantage of your child's vulnerabilities.

Hence, it's imperative for you as parents to maintain a good friendship with your teenager, be there for them & help them differentiate between good and bad.

3. Others:

Such as teachers, counselors, coaches, and mentors can offer advice, guidance, and support from a neutral viewpoint or specialized advice based on their professional experience. In shaping the lives of many great men, teachers have played a pivotal role, even when parents were not there.

When a teen has a strong support system, it helps them deal with stress in a positive way, learn from their experiences and emerge stronger for future challenges.

But when they don't have the right support system, it can prove very harmful - causing loneliness, fear, insecurity, low self-confidence, low self-esteem, chronic physical & mental diseases, learning difficulties, behavioral disturbances, etc.

Remember, all teens are different and some types of help might work better than others in a particular child. The important thing is, they should be confident they are not alone.

In the next 2 chapters, we will talk about the most important 2 external support systems for a teenager to overcome their stress: parents and friends.

Meanwhile, I have homework for you here - two questions.

Your page

1. **Whom do your teens reach out to first, when stressed?**

2. **How do you handle your own stress? What do you do?**

Chapter 19

Parents - friends or foes

Parents ought to play a crucial role in supporting their children throughout their childhood.

And this support becomes all the more crucial during teenage.

I have some steps for you (parents) about what to do when your teen looks distressed:

- this time, instead of dismissing their stress, sit down with them, ask what's bothering them, and genuinely listen (remember what we all discussed regarding open communication)
- show them that you understand (& do everything possible to actually understand); listen from that space of concern & empathy
- acknowledge their feelings
- don't brush off their concerns without actually listening to them

Sometimes, all they need is someone to hear them out, and who better than you?

- Let your teenager know that it's okay to feel stressed. We all do at times.
- The important thing is how we handle it.
- Share your own experiences with stress and offer them helpful tips (by the way, did you write about how you handle your own stress). But don't bog them down narrating your experiences. The present issue is about them, not you. So, maintain a balance while sharing your experiences.
- Being a good role model is very important. It has a bigger impact than you realize.

Remember, being a parent is not just about providing material things. Equally important is:

- Guiding them through the ups & downs of life, &
- Being there with them in circumstances, when nothing else seems to work and only time holds the power to heal

One piece of caution for you here:

- In the present superfast era of over ambition, achieving more & more, & hyper stimulation (from virtual world to superfast food to streetlights to signboards to movies to web series to what not), parents, instead of becoming a part of the support system of their teenagers, maybe unknowingly becoming a part of their stresses

- This is one thing which all parents must take care to avoid
- **Learn to be their friends while still being their parents**
- & Give them a strong conviction that, no matter what, you are there for your son, your daughter

Simply being with them reduces their stress; just this acknowledgement that there is someone I can depend on, goes a long way in protecting them from the stress & its ill effects, helping them emerge victorious & stronger.

The next chapter is about Friends, Friendships & Peer Pressure.

Again, in today's era, friends can become a strong pillar of support for each other but can also become a potent source of stress. How to be aware of & handle this is what we will see next.

Chapter 20

Friends, Friendships & Peer Pressure

As children grow, they naturally become attracted to other children their age, developing friendships with some & differences with others.

For younger kids, parents are still more important even as they make new friends, but as they grow 8-10 years old and beyond, the importance of their friends starts becoming more than their parents.

- Is this happening to you?
- Do you feel hurt due to this?
- Don't, it's normal.
- It's actually good.

Making friends is a normal part of growing up.

In fact, if your children, especially teenagers, don't have friends, then it's a matter of concern.

We, as parents, should help our children in developing healthy friendships.

But, along with friendships, there comes peer pressure, where friends influence each other to do certain things or behave in a certain specific way.

- This peer pressure can be positive when friends encourage each other to make good choices or encourage healthy competition.
- However, there can also be negative peer pressure, where friends influence each other to engage in risky or harmful behaviors like smoking, drinking, drugs, criminal activities, rash driving, etc.
- One particularly distressing problem in our society today is substance abuse, like the use of recreational drugs. Substance abuse often starts innocuously, with the majority being introduced to drugs by their peers.
- Curiosity, the desire for fun and the urge to fit in the peer group can lead children down this dangerous path.

Dealing with peer pressure can be tough, especially in today's overtly comparison oriented & technology-driven world.

Please note - courage, confidence & ability to say NO without hurting is a critical skill that every teen must learn & nurture in their life.

- As we will discuss in the coming chapters, when a teen has Self-Awareness & has learned how to handle their emotions, it immensely boosts their self-esteem & self-confidence.
- This self-confidence provides them with the needed strength to say "NO" to unhealthy peer pressure.
- With a high self-esteem, they are able to tactfully & firmly decline peer pressure instead of caving into it.
- Parents have a big role to play in developing this self-esteem & self-confidence.

Another very important thing - don't look forward to making your teens submissive. If you want your children to always say YES to everything you say, then that becomes their habit & there's a high chance they'll also be saying YES to everything their peers are suggesting, whether right or wrong, safe or risky.

Mind-blowing - isn't it? Ever thought that way?

When I read this for the first time in my life, my eyes went wide open. I had never thought about it like this before. Are you also feeling this way? Good!

So, when you respect your children well, encourage open discussion & allow them to say NO to you, you help them develop a habit of critically analyzing the available options before agreeing to one.

Then this becomes a natural habit for them before saying YES to anything & they develop the strength to say NO whenever needed.

Conviction & ability to say NO - an important critical life skill - for boys; for girls; for you; for me; for everyone.

Remember, Life skills and Spirituality are protective factors in life - for boys; for girls; for you; for me; for everyone.

Life skills form the internal support system & are the tools everyone needs to deal with the everyday life challenges in a healthy way.

We will talk about them in the next chapter.

Your page

Write the names of friends of your son & daughter & what you like or dislike about them

Friend 1: ....

1. ____
2. ____
3. ____
4. ____
5. ____

Friend 2: ....

1. ____
2. ____
3. ____
4. ____
5. ____

Chapter 21

Teen's Internal Support System - the Life Skills

We may not be able to prepare the future for our children, but we can prepare our children for the future - said Franklin D. Roosevelt, in a letter dated September 17, 1938.

And the statement holds true even now, even after almost a hundred years.

- The goal is NOT - to prevent all adversities & stress from coming into our children's lives.
- The goal is - to empower them with the skills they need to handle these adversities & stresses

Life skills are the essential abilities that help one face the small & big challenges & stresses of life in a positive way and emerge stronger.

- They are like superpowers that our kids can use whenever they need them, like life jackets to be used whenever the waters become too deep.

- With these skills, they develop perseverance, resilience, adaptability & can bounce back from tough situations in life.

Let's look at the '10 core Life-skills' as suggested by the WHO:

- Decision-making
- Problem-solving
- Creative thinking
- Critical thinking
- Effective communication
- Interpersonal relationship skills
- Self-awareness
- Empathy
- Coping with emotions
- Coping with stress

Some important points:

- Self-Awareness is said to be the most crucial skill. As one masters Self-Awareness, all other critical skills follow automatically.
- Suicide is among the top 2 causes of death in the teenage years. Reason - Inability to handle their emotions & stress.
- Someone who has Self-Awareness & has learned to handle their emotions & stresses well is unlikely to

take such extreme steps like suicide, running away, succumbing to peer pressure, indulging in antisocial activities, etc.

- And these Life skills are not just for children or teens, but for people of all ages.

The question is, how to inculcate these life skills in our teens?

Inculcating life skills in teens can be achieved through a combination of various strategies:

- Being good role models: Parents apply these skills in their own lives. Teens see & learn.
- Providing practical opportunities for teenagers to apply the skills in real life situations without fear of failure.
- Encouraging them to make decisions and solve problems without worrying too much about the outcomes. You may begin with low stake issues.
- Participation in team sports and other group activities like traveling, hiking, etc.
- Leadership and volunteer role in school and community organizations.
- Personality development books and articles.
- Targeted workshops - offline or online

Remember, inculcating life skills is a gradual process that requires patience and consistency. Being a good role model helps a lot.

Provide ongoing support, encouragement, and guidance to help teenagers develop these skills, and celebrate their failures, victories & progress along the way.

Our ancient (yet ever new) Science of Yoga, Pranayama & Meditation is the most effective way for inculcating & nurturing various life skills, including Self-awareness, ability to cope with emotions & stress, developing good communication skills, self-confidence, self-esteem, critical thinking skills, creativity, curiosity, empathy, & others.

Since, along with being a Pediatrician, I am also a GOI Ayush Mantralaya certified Yoga teacher, & specially trained to take the teachings of Yogic science to children & teenagers (in a language they would understand & appreciate), I have included a full chapter on how the teachings of Yogic Science can help today's teenagers, in this book.

But before we embark on that, I want to talk about the most important & probably the most neglected person in your life – YOU.

Chapter 22

Secure your Oxygen mask first

TAKE CARE of YOURSELF

Dear friend,

Along with the role of a mother or a father, you must be playing so many other roles in your life & might have so many other responsibilities along with caring for your teens, like taking care of your job, your aging parents, your own health, financial challenges, uncertainties in life, etc. And certainly, this can be overwhelming.

Are you looking well after yourself?

As we reach this stage in our book, I want to emphasize the importance of taking good care of yourself as an individual. You need a lot of energy to do justice to all of your responsibilities. Therefore, it's all the more important that you don't forget your own well-being. Just like on an airplane, you are told to secure your own oxygen mask first before assisting anybody else, even before your toddler.

Look, if you don't take good care of yourself, how are you going to take good care of your near and dear ones for long?

Possible challenges you may face with your own care may be:

- difficulty finding time
- lack of support
- not knowing exactly what to do
- struggling to maintain consistency

But I feel the most important reason is: Not really understanding the value of self-care & prioritizing oneself.

I will say it again. Look, if you don't take good care of yourself, how are you going to take good care of your teenage son & daughter & other near and dear ones for long? It's time to wake up for YOU.

And let's not get confused, prioritizing oneself doesn't mean neglecting others. It means getting the best of both worlds. Because, when you attend to yourself, you have more energy, patience, and resilience to carry out all other responsibilities in a better way, including supporting and guiding your teenager.

And when you do good self-care, you become a good role model too.

Ask yourself, **ARE YOU A GOOD ROLE MODEL:**

- Do you tend to lose your cool often?
- How committed are you in your words & acts?
- How much do you yourself follow the values which you want to see in your children, like eating well, exercising well, sleeping & waking up on time, respecting elders, healthy gadgets use, etc.?
- How much do you do those same things which you tell your teens not to, like screen time, social media, web series, etc.?

Because you ought to first practice, what you preach. Only preaching doesn't work with children. And for this, you ought to have more patience & energy level. Don't you agree?

So, make sure to take out time for activities that bring you joy and relaxation. And remember, it's okay to take help when you need it.

I regularly conduct online yoga classes for teens & for adults too. You may opt to join either of them. Joining along with your spouse & teens would be a particularly good idea. That will become a quality family time too, along with rejuvenation for all of you together. A practice of yogic science, breathing, yognidra, meditation has the capacity to totally transform one's whole life.

My best wishes to you. May you take very good care of yourself, and embrace the beautiful journey of parenthood with love and joy.

In our next chapter, I'll summarize all the key aspects in the lives of your teenage sons and daughters which you need to pay attention to, along with some eye-opening data.

Chapter 23

Exploring Key Aspects and Important Data

During adolescence, the body undergoes significant changes. This time is crucial for developing a strong foundation for lifelong health.

From the age 10-19 years, a teenager gains:

- about 20% of their total height
- about 50% of their total weight
- up to 40% of their adult bone mass

Teenage is the last opportunity for teenagers to achieve their full potential in terms of physical development, including height, weight, and bone mass. If they don't get proper nutrition, exercise, sleep and support during this time, a teen might not reach their full growth potential & can have long-lasting adverse effects on their overall health.

In this chapter, we dive into some key aspects of today's teenager's lives and uncover some relevant eye-opening data. My intention is to make you realize the gravity of the situation and encourage you to take the required action.

1. Academic pressure

Research shows that this is the most pressing stressor both for parents and their teens.

I earnestly wish to tell you that strict, authoritarian parenting and undue academic pressure is one of the most common cause of suicidal attempts among teens in the Indian subcontinent today.

And suicide is one of the top two most common causes of death in teens.

How to find the balance between encouraging a teenager for academic excellence and avoiding undue pressure is the question every parent must seek an answer to? What would be the best choice of career for your teen is another important thing to think well about.

Life skills are life jackets here too.

2. Technology and social media

Technology is a boon. Technology is a curse. All depends on, how we use it.

The unhealthy use of social media and technology is severely impacting our teenager's mental, physical and emotional health today (& ours too).

Inadvertent exposure to pornography is resulting in a casual attitude towards physical relationships, even creating complications in married life later. Managing technology and optimizing social media use is a critical skill for both teenagers and their parents today.

I call it **'The Today's Chakravyuh'.** Even a one-year-old child knows how to enter it, but does anyone know how to exit?? I intend to soon write a guidebook for parents on this crucial topic.

3. Food & Eating

Researchers have proved that only 1 out of 10 teens is eating the minimum required adequate diet today (UNICEF Survey 2019). And a vast majority of them have one or other nutritional deficiency today.

Unhealthy eating & overweight/obesity are directly linked to diseases such as Diabetes, Hypertension (high BP), heart attacks and at least 13 types of cancers apart from decreased quality of life, low self-esteem, suboptimal mental health & many other issues.

Obesity rates have doubled in recent years & are increasing at an alarming rate. It's an epidemic today. As a result, these diseases are spreading rapidly, affecting even younger people today.

The increasing incidence of chronic diseases and the decreasing ability to fight infectious infections can be largely attributed to the unhealthy lifestyle choices we make, including our diet.

It's high time we start paying serious attention to what we & our children are eating.

I soon intend to write a couple of books on this topic:

- one on authentic & easy to apply tips for parents which will immediately decrease their headache regarding the eating attitude of their children (of all ages), &
- one book on how to address the unhealthy gain in weight in teenagers & regain their health & fitness

4. Physical activity & Sleep

Come on, so many things to do - school, tuition, homework, coaching, tests .... & TV, video games, social media ....

Where is the time to play? ... & to sleep?

But, no matter what, adequate physical activity and sleep are non-negotiable for good memory, for good marks, for creativity, for success, for physical health, for mental health, for enthusiasm, for vigor, for a good quality of life, for everything.

Even when preparing for tough competitive exams, some physical activity in any form is a must & will only enhance your teen's results.

AND 8-9-10 hours of deep, uninterrupted sleep (preferably following the circadian rhythm) is an absolute must for every teenager. If you want them to excel in life, including their exams, & still be physically & mentally strong & fit, ensure they sleep well & enough.

A message for teens: If you want to reduce your number of hours of sleep without compromising on your health & productivity, so that you can do more, add some physical activity, some yoga, some pranayama, & some meditation in your life. Yog nidra can be another big savior.

5. Sexual health & Sexuality concerns

This big elephant has been sitting in the room for a long, long time now & needs to be addressed without any further delay. Lack of a proper guidance regarding this topic causes a lot of stress in teens.

When parents talk about these sensitive topics with their children in a proper manner, it is protective for the children & also helps in opening up a new window of deeper relationship based on trust & mutual respect.

Some facts for you:

- Proper sex education does not lead to an increase in or early sexual experiments/indulgences in adolescents; rather, research has shown again and again that whenever proper, relevant sex education is given in communities, the incidences of teenage pregnancies, abortions, and STIs have gone down significantly.
- Boys need more help as compared to girls, because girls, being emotionally closer to their parents, can

talk about this subject with their mother, but boys are unlikely to be able to talk about it with their parents.

- Most teens who indulge in unprotected sex are not aware of the fact that pregnancies can occur as a result of sex.

Proper sexual education has become all the more important today in the wake of digital media & the easy availability of misleading information & rampant pornography therein.

6. Mental health

Last but not the least, mental health problems aren't just for adults.

Recently WHO & other agencies did surveys in India - they found that almost 40-45% of Indian children below the age of 18 years are facing some or other mental or behavioral issues; & this figure is increasing day by day.

Today, issues like anxiety, depression, and stress are common among teenagers & young adults too.

15% or more teens suffer from anxiety & 5% or more from depression & this may well be an understatement, the large majority going undiagnosed & unnoticed, suffering in silence.

Most issues begin with behavioral changes & when not addressed in time or properly enough, tend to aggravate into more problematic mental & psychiatric ones.

Yet, unfortunately, most cases go undetected and untreated until later, because:

- Parents often don't notice the problems or tend to neglect them until late
- Mental health issues often don't receive the same attention as physical health issues
- Teens often don't openly discuss topics like sex, drugs, or mental health
- Teenagers often feel embarrassed or ashamed to admit they need help
- Teenagers often don't seek help unless their friends suggest
- Communication gap of teens with parents & other adults - no one to talk to

Parents, most of these problems can be avoided, minimized or addressed & rectified.

Paying proper attention to these six key areas can bring about an unbelievable transformation in the life of your teen.

Chapter 24

The Science of Yoga for teenagers

Neither at home nor in school are we taught:

- how to handle our emotions
- how to cope when we feel sad / angry / frustrated / cheated

Rather, in many instances, we are discouraged even from expressing our emotions, perceiving it as a sign of weakness.

Result: growing up this way, all our lives, we keep struggling to cope with our emotions & stress & don't know what to do.

The science of yoga tells us that our breath is directly connected with our emotions. When we are angry or sad or depressed or agitated or happy, in each of these different states of mind, our breath is also different. When our state of mind changes, the rhythm of our breath also changes.

But this relationship is not just one way, it works both ways. We can consciously change the rhythm of our breath to change our emotions & the state of our mind. **This is a secret** & a regular practice of this secret through Pranayamas can do wonders for strengthening the emotional & mental health of our teens. We read in **Ch 16** about the numerous stressors during the teenage years. The science of yoga offers an excellent solution to all these challenges facing our teens.

Let's look at some key areas in which our teens can reap great benefits from the practice of Yogic science in their lives:

- Emotional stability & balance
- Skill to cope with emotional turmoil, anxiety, feelings of low, mood swings
- Mental clarity & strength
- Focus, concentration, memory, learning & unlearning
- Quality of Sleep
- Acceptance of self & others
- Relationships with friends & family
- Decision-making, fewer confusions
- Greater flexibility, strength and overall agility in the body

- Improved posture and balance, with reduced stiffness
- Self-management, time-management & self-discipline
- Self-confidence, self-worth & will-power
- Combating pressures (academic, peer & others)
- A positive attitude toward life's challenges
- Facing failure or rejection
- Self-awareness & intuition, a deeper understanding of oneself - what I want from my life

In the Ch 5, we talked about “the accelerator system” & “the brake system” in a teenager’s brain. A proper practice of Yogic science can greatly facilitate the maturity of the prefrontal cortex of their brain, strengthening their brake system & reduce the hyperactivity of their accelerator system.

Yoga strengthens the conscious connections between the basal ganglia, the limbic system & the neocortex parts of the brain, enhancing the Self-awareness of an individual. And as we talked in Ch 21, Self-awareness is the fundamental life skill that serves as a mother skill for the development of all other skills.

Regular meditation & deep relaxation has been shown to reduce the size of amygdale in brain which is the seat of hot cognition & emotional hyperactivity.

I have mentioned only some of the numerous benefits proper Yogic practices can confer. However, it is essential to always initiate Yogic practices under the guidance of a trained facilitator to ensure proper technique and safety.

There is a science to Yoga & then there is also an Art to it. There are some subtle yet significant elements that can profoundly enhance one's practice and yield greater benefits. Even if a teen dedicates a short span of time to the practice of Yogic science, paying attention to these subtle aspects can yield significant benefits for them.

The time & effort they invest in, is sure to be repaid many times over in their lives in numerous ways.

Chapter 25

And the story of 4 painters

A beautiful story very close to my heart.

Once upon a time, not so far away, there was a happy kingdom ruled by a one-eyed (काना) King. To immortalize himself, he thought of getting his painting drawn and made an announcement all over the kingdom with an Oscar for the best portrait.

There were 3 exceptional painters in that kingdom, who took the challenge. Afterall, the Oscar was at stake.

But the king was one-eyed. So, what to do?

Painter no 1 thought:

- **"Why take chances?** If I draw his portrait with only one eye good & the other eye blind and the King gets furious, he might even hang me? And besides, my portrait will be there long after the king has gone."

- **Result:** he painted the portrait of the king, an exact replica, but with both eyes good.

Painter no 2 said:

- **"I don't care.** I will stick with the fact as it is, no matter the consequences. The king is one eyed so his portrait should also show him like that. That's not my fault. It's the way things are."
- **Result:** he painted the portrait of the king, an exact replica, & blind with one eye.

Painter no 3 contemplated:

- **"What can I do so that** I stick with the truth too and at the same time don't hurt the king? He thought and found a way."
- **Result:** he drew the portrait of the King, an exact replica, hunting with his bow and arrow, taking aim with the good eye and the blind eye closed.

& The Oscar goes to? - No awards for guessing the winner - Painter no 3.

And then there was also a **fourth category** of painters, those who didn't even turn up to take the challenge, who were lost in their own world & bothered neither about the painting nor about the king.

Friends, similarly there are four types of parents.

Parents like painter number 1:

- Such parents look to avoid any type of uncomfortable situation, any type of confrontation with their children, and end up being goody-goody with them all the time. And they come up with very fine excuses for their choice of actions.
- **Result:** Children of such parents throw a lot of tantrums & get their demands fulfilled by hook or by crook. These children, as they grow, fail to learn to live a disciplined life or to hear a NO from someone; they can't face failure or rejection. They grow up feeling unsupported and insecure.

Parents like painter number 2:

- Such parents are very strict & don't allow much space or relaxation to their children, and may even give physical punishment for disciplining them.
- **Result:** Children of such parents fear them & fail to develop an emotional connection & bond with them. Such children fail to develop self-confidence & self-esteem. Though at a young age, such children live in forced discipline, as they grow, they tend to become either rebellious & aggressive or withdrawn & submissive.

Parents like painter number 3:

- This is a relatively rare variety, a good combination of being firm & being relaxed too. These are the winner parents, who communicate the truth, yet are careful about the way they do that. They give time to find such solutions that सांप भी मर जाए और लाठी भी ना टूटे, that they may have the cake and eat it too.

- **Result:** Children of such parents learn discipline while also developing a deep emotional connection, bonding and respect for their parents. They grow up feeling supported and protected. Such children have the confidence to take initiative in life, be intuitive and resilient.

Parents like the fourth category of painters:

- They hardly participate in the upbringing of their children.
- **Result:** These children fail to develop any connection, bonding or respect for such parents & grow feeling lonely & unsupported. How they fare in their life is entirely dependent on other circumstances & factors. Such children are more vulnerable to external pressures, have low confidence, low self-esteem, and struggle in school or any other team activities & are liable to develop behavioral & psychological issues.

The children of all the four types of parents carry on this learned legacy to their own children & family & the cycle continues, until someone wakes up & takes the required steps for their children's betterment.

Ever thought - What's your type?

- If you belong to the **type 1** category, it would do you good to develop more firmness in your communication. You have to learn to say NO to your teens & set boundaries.
- If you belong to the **type 2** category, it would do you good to be a little more relaxed & shower more love. You have to practice taking it easy.
- If you belong to **type 4,** chances are very less that you would even read this book
- And if you belong to the **type 3** category, congratulations. Keep learning new things & keep improving. **The Oscar is yours.**

And remember that you need to keep learning as a parent in order to be able to teach & guide your teens. It's like regularly upgrading your own software & keeping installing the latest antivirus to face the ever new & emerging threats of the newer generations.

As we come to the end of our book, I want to express my gratitude for your commitment and participation. It has been a pleasure sharing myself with you, and I hope that the information and insights provided in the book have proved useful to you.

See you in the next book

Best wishes

Epilogue

Every beginning has an end & every end has a beginning.

By taking the initiative to understand various aspects of your teen's lives and seeking ways to support them, you can make a remarkable difference in their life. I wish the best to you & your teens in your endeavors.

We discussed so many things along the way.

I hope they have helped you with easing your problems.

Let's summarize what we discussed & learned:

1. Which type of parent you are (Ch 25)
2. Your main challenges regarding your teenage son/daughter (Ch 2)
3. The main reasons behind the way teens act (Ch 4, 5)
4. The stressors in the life of a teen (Ch 16)
5. Mistakes in handling teen's stresses (Ch 17)
6. Teens don't listen - Why (Ch 12)
7. Some eye-opening data regarding teenagers today (Ch 23)

8. And we also talked about the steps needed to solve your issues with your teen & achieve your desired result:
    - The most important aspect - strengthening your connection with your child - Quality Time (Ch 9, 10, 11)
    - The Golden Formula - You & your teens are one team (Ch 1)
    - Feeling & saying sorry, reversing the wheel of hurt (Ch 8)
    - Optimizing communication (Ch 13, 14)
    - The power of physical touch (Ch 15)
    - Teaching your teens how to handle stress & peer pressure - supportive atmosphere (Ch 18, 19, 20) & teaching them the Life skills (Ch 21)
    - Giving due importance to self-care (Ch 22)
    - The super transformation the teachings of Yogic science can bring in the teens (Ch 24)
    - & Some real-life stories (Ch 3, 6, 7)

I sincerely hope that the insights shared in this book have provided you with valuable guidance, practical strategies, and a fresh perspective on nurturing your teenagers. Remember, the challenges you may face along the way are part of the growth process, and you are not alone in this journey. By supporting and learning from one another, we can create a nurturing community that fosters positive relationships with our teenagers.

As we conclude this book, I encourage you to reflect on your learning and continue implementing the strategies and techniques that resonate with you. Remember to adapt them to your unique family dynamics.

And most importantly, be kind to yourself. Parenting is a journey filled with ups and downs, and it's important to celebrate your successes and acknowledge the efforts you put into your role as a parent.

Once again, thank you for being a part of this journey and for your dedication to your teenager's well-being. If you have any further questions or need additional support, please don't hesitate to reach out by writing to me at admin@optimumparenting.com

Wishing you and your teens a life of continued growth, joy, success and resilience.

With heartfelt gratitude & blessings

Dr. B B Agrawal (MD)

About the author

My name is **Banke Bihari Agrawal.**
(Given by my late dadaji).

And I am:

- a consulting Pediatrician by profession
- a passionate parent's guide with 20+ years of experience in dealing with children, teens & their parents
- a certified Yoga teacher
- an author & content creator

My educational & other qualifications:

- MBBS, MD (Pediatrics), IMS, BHU
- Director - Shiv Shakti Hospital, Bilaspur (C.G.)

- Founder - Optimum Parenting Mission
- Guiding teenagers & their parents for 20+ years in my hospital & conducting parenting workshops for parents of younger children & teens since 2010.
- Certified by SSU, Cuttack for Counseling & CBT techniques for anxiety, depression & stress.
- Govt. of India, Ayush Mantralaya Certified Yoga trainer (& a Yoga enthusiast).
- Specially trained to take the benefits of Yogic Science to Children & Teenagers in a language they would understand & appreciate.

Resources

- Twitter link: https://x.com/agrawaldrbb
- YouTube channel – Dr B B Agrawal Parent's Guide - YouTube
- https://optimumparenting.com/ (under process)
- Mummy papa website (https://mummypapa.online/) & mummy papa App (for android at present) - for pregnant ladies & new parents - breastfeeding, development & nurturing intelligence in young babies, day-today confusion & care for newborns & young babies. Free access.

YouTube

Twitter

Mummy Papa APP
(free access)

MUMMY PAPA
The art of bringing up

Other / Upcoming books

- A book on day today issues which parents face regarding food & eating of their children with authentic & easy to apply tips which will immediately decrease their headache;
- A book on how to address the unhealthy weight gain in teenagers & regain their health & fitness
- A book on screen & teens
- A book on discipline & teens
- More books, depending on the feedback about this book we get from you & inputs on what you want to know more about

What Next

We have created a dedicated community for sincere parents of teenage children where:

- we discuss various issues parents & their teenagers are struggling with
- conduct webinars, &
- workshops to solve those problems
- both parents & their teenagers are involved in sessions
- both free & paid sessions are there

The entry in the community is completely free & by invitation only. If you are interested in becoming a part of this community, please email us at admin@optimumparenting.com with subject line as **Interested** & we will send you the interest form.

Your Space

****